THE OCEAN CITY
NEW JERSEY
BUCKET LIST

100 WAYS TO HAVE A REAL OCEAN CITY EXPERIENCE

D1495359

MARY ANN BOLEN

ISBN-13:
978-1475296051

ISBN-10:
1475296053

If you would like to write a "Bucket List" about your area, contact me at MaryAnn.Bolen@gmail.com and I will be happy to help you get started.

legal disclaimer

This book is designed to provide information, entertainment, and motivation to our readers. It is sold with the understanding that the publisher is not engaged to render any type of physical, psychological, legal, or any other kind of professional advice.

Participation in the activities listed may be dangerous or illegal and could lead to arrest, serious injury, or death.

The content of this book is the sole expression and opinion of its author and not necessarily that of the publisher. No warranties or guarantees are expressed or implied.

Neither the publisher nor the individual author shall be liable for any physical, psychological, emotional, financial, or commercial damages, including, but not limited to, special, incidental, consequential, or other damages.

Our views and rights are the same: you are responsible for your own choices, actions, and results.

dedication

To my husband, BOB, my best friend, my lover, my "stalker" and my tech department. His ideas, wit, encouragement and computer skills made it possible for me to share this book with you, and I could not have done it without him. Love you.

To my family, KEVIN, PAM, MANDY, STAN, JACK, ANDREW, who actually started this book one summer morning around the kitchen table while discussing David Sloan's *The Key West Bucket List*.

When I casually mentioned, "I could write a book like this," they handed me a pen and paper, and so the list began. Their contributions, personal favorites, editing skills, encouragement, humor and support were essential and much appreciated. Love you.

acknowledgements

Thank you to *The Key West Bucket List* author, David Sloan, whose book was the inspiration behind *The Ocean City Bucket List*. His guidance helping this first time author was truly appreciated. Thanks, David, for allowing me to be the first to add my hometown to The Bucket List series.

Thank you to Danette Baso Silvers, graphic designer, who expertly took a word document and some vague layout ideas and created this wonderful book.

If you would like to write a "Bucket List" about your area, contact me at MaryAnn.Bolen@gmail.com and I will be happy to help you get started.

why a bucket list?

I was chatting on our porch one recent summer with a woman who's been vacationing here for more than 40 years. Like me, she had watched her kids graduate from sand toys to surfboards and carousels to curfews.

She had seen and done all the usual things, but had only scratched the surface. Ocean City is more than beach days and boardwalk nights, much more. There were things she never knew existed, but that shouldn't be missed.

Have you ever:

- seen the "doll houses" on Wovern Place?
- bought ½ price ride tickets?
- explored the alleyways?
- pedaled along the Haven Avenue Bike Path?

Ocean City has hidden gems not found in any guidebooks, not advertised on any brochures. This book takes you behind the scenes of our favorite city. Some of the entries may be familiar, and you can check those off immediately, but others may be a mystery.

As you check off your adventures (some easy, some more challenging), you'll have the satisfaction of knowing you've gone beyond the typical "tourist" status and become an "honorary local," and trust me, that's a more desirable handle than "shoobie."

Like kids at the beach, we should all dig deeper, and once you hit water, you'll truly know the town we love. I hope this book will help you to "feel" what makes Ocean City so special to me and my family.

1

grab the brass ring on the carousel and win a free ride

DID YOU KNOW????
Wonderland Pier opened in 1965.

2

enjoy a slice at Manco & Manco's (formerly Mack & Manco) counter and watch the pizza gurus toss the dough

3

take an outside shower

WORTH REPEATING...
"Bing Crosby sings like all people
think they sing in the shower."
Dinah Shore

4

win a free game
of miniature golf
on the last hole

5

crash a
Night In Venice
party on the bay

6

critique other people's parallel parking skills from your porch

7

confiscate all
video games and
play a marathon
game of Monopoly
on a rainy day

8

watch the July 4th fireworks from the beach

9

find a live crab in the rocks on the jetty

10

eat a Jersey tomato

WORTH REPEATING...
"Knowledge is knowing a tomato is a fruit;
Wisdom is not putting it in a fruit salad."
Author unknown

11

have your picture
taken on the
lifeguard stand at
your favorite beach

DID YOU KNOW????
James Stewart, actor, spent summers
here during his childhood.

12

try to finish a large
Voltaco's cheese
steak by yourself

13

stay inside the green flags on protected beaches

14

fish from the old Longport Bridge

15

ride a surrey cart
on the boardwalk
and let the youngest
take the wheel

16

buy an original piece from the artist at the Boardwalk Art Show

17

test your relationship on a bicycle built for two

WORTH REPEATING...
"Get a bicycle. You will not regret it. If you live."
Mark Twain

18

take a stroll and shop on Asbury Avenue

19

ask them to overflow the bucket at Johnson's Popcorn ("lid off")

DID YOU KNOW????
There once was a roller skating rink
on Atlantic Avenue near 1st Street.

20

make a drip castle

21

see the island from the top of the Wonderland Ferris Wheel

WORTH REPEATING...
"I see nothing in space as promising
as the view from a Ferris wheel."
E. B. White

22

read all of the boardwalk bench dedications

23

buy a kite at
Air Circus on the
boardwalk and fly
it on the beach

24

forget your age
and have fun at
the boardwalk rides

WORTH REPEATING...
"At some point in your life, if you're lucky,
you throw practicality to the
wind and start living."
Erma Bombeck

25

finish a Kohr Bros.
soft serve cone
with "jimmies"
(yes, they are
called jimmies,
not sprinkles)
before it melts

WORTH REPEATING...
"Age does not diminish the extreme disappointment
of having a scoop of ice cream fall from the cone."
Jim Fiebig

26

take a surfing lesson

27

arrange for a delivery from Circle Liquor Store

WORTH REPEATING...
"It's a good idea to obey all the rules when you're young just so you'll have the strength to break them when you're old."
Mark Twain

28

explore
Ocean City's alleys

29

attempt to save
a parking spot
on the street using
only your body

30

shop the Farmer's Market on Wednesday mornings at the Tabernacle

31

find the perfect
shell and bring it
home for someone

32

enjoy a warm donut
or two from Brown's
on the boardwalk

33

lose yourself
in a good book
on the beach

DID YOU KNOW????
Gay Talese, author, grew up in Ocean City
and still vacations here.

34

help a stranger
save their
belongings before
getting washed out
at high tide

35

keep repeating,
"I'm on vacation,
I'm on vacation,"
while driving
around looking for
a parking space

36

find a treasure
at a yard sale

DID YOU KNOW????
The ship Sindia sunk in 1901
off the 17th Street beach on its way
to New York City from Kobe, Japan.

37

take an
Inn to Inn Tour

DID YOU KNOW????
Alden Park Manor in the north end
had rooms for $15 a night in the '60s
and a room with a bath was $35 a night in 1976.

38

watch the
Baby Parade
on the boardwalk
(the oldest
in the U.S.)

WORTH REPEATING…
"Did you know babies are nauseated
by the smell of a clean shirt?"
Jeff Foxworthy

39

try some chicken salad from Bakley's Deli

40

watch them pull the salt water taffy at Shriver's

DID YOU KNOW????
The Wrigley Family, founders of Wrigley Gum,
once had a summer home in the Gardens

41

find the "doll houses" on Wovern Place

WORTH REPEATING...
"Simplicity is the ultimate sophistication."
Leonardo DaVinci

42

learn to body surf

43

find out the origin of the word "shoobie"

44

race across hot sand
without shoes

45

ride a bike from one end of the boardwalk to the other

46

have breakfast overlooking the ocean at Oves

47

walk on the beach in
the early morning
and be the first
to leave footprints
in the sand

48

take a photo of the sun rising over the ocean

49

play paddleball
or have a game
of catch by the water

50

take your shoes
off and stroll on
the beach in the
evening

51

take a trolley ride the length of the island

DID YOU KNOW????
There were three salt-water pools
in front of the Flanders Hotel.

52

bring home a dozen
Mallon's sticky buns
for the family;
that way, **_you_** get
to choose nut,
plain, raisin
or fruit flavored

53

attend First Night
celebration
including the
fireworks
at midnight

54

check out
the lagoons via
wave runners

DID YOU KNOW????
Chris' Restaurant had four surplus WWII PT boats – three were
fishing boats: The Wild Goose, The Flying Cloud, The Gone
With the Wind. The Flying Saucer took sightseers for a high
speed ride from 1953 to 1970.

55

walk from one end of the boardwalk to the other

DID YOU KNOW????
In the 1920's, people never went to the boardwalk
without wearing their Sunday best.

56

dig in the dry sand
until you reach
water or run
out of arm

57

find the late Grace Kelly's old family home

58

adopt a hermit crab and name him Hermie

59

start a yearly beach tag collection

DID YOU KNOW????
Beach tags started in 1976,
when a season tag was $5.

60

get creamy fudge from the kettles at Fudge Kitchen

61

spend an hour just
people watching
on the boardwalk

62

hang out on the porch; leave all the electronics inside

63

treat yourself to your
favorite junk food
on the boardwalk —
you're on vacation

64

surf fish
from the beach

65

enjoy a toe-tapping
musical evening at
the Music Pier with
the Ocean City Pops

DID YOU KNOW????
The Music Pier opened 1929.

66

protect your lunch on the beach from a seagull attack

67

take a ride on the Haven Avenue bike path

68

introduce yourself to the folks on the porch next door

69

buy ½ price ride
tickets on
Palm Sunday
and Easter Sunday
weekends

DID YOU KNOW????
The Ferris Wheel was the first
ride at Gillian's Fun Deck.

70

share an order of wings at Charlie's Bar in Somers Point

71

go to the beach
with only a towel,
a chair and a book

72

peruse the latest selections at Sun Rose Words & Music in town

WORTH REPEATING...
"There is more treasure in books than
in all the pirate's loot on Treasure Island."
Walt Disney

73

take your dog for a
swim at Dog Beach
and a romp at the
Dog Park

74

walk across
the new causeway
from Ocean City
to Somers Point

75

buy an Ocean City
hat or shirt
to wear at home

76

catch a sand crab,
give it to a little kid
and listen to
them squeal

77

let the water lap
at your ankles
as you stand at
water's edge
and talk with
family/friends

78

leave work
at home and
lose track of what
day of the week it is

79

be the first
on the beach
to spot the dolphins
swimming offshore

WORTH REPEATING...
"Did you know that dolphins are so smart that within a few
weeks of captivity, they can train people to stand on the very
edge of the pool and throw them fish?"
Author unknown

80

smile and say "Hi"
to strangers
when they pass

81

attend a church
service of a
denomination
different than
your own

82

turn off the a/c,
open the windows
and feel the
ocean breeze

83

visit Ocean City after a snowfall — a true winter wonderland

DID YOU KNOW????
Wonderland Pier used to flood
the inside for ice skating.

84

take a nap
on the beach

85

wash out a cut or
scrape in the ocean
while expounding
on the healing
powers of salt water

86

take a bike ride through the Gardens

WORTH REPEATING...
"Life is like riding a bicycle. Most of us
have gears we never use."
Charles Shultz

87

watch a
thunderstorm
from the shelter
of your porch

88

lose track of time as you walk along the water's edge from beach to beach

89

visit Corson's Inlet
State Park in the
south end of town

90

say thanks to the lifeguard at the end of your visit

DID YOU KNOW????
The award winning Ocean City Beach Patrol
(OCBP) has been protecting us since 1898.

91

take a ½ day fishing
trip and try to win
the pool

WORTH REPEATING...
"The gods do not deduct from man's
allotted span the hours spent fishing."
Proverb

92

eat Jersey sweet
corn on the cob
and compare it
to prior seasons

93

respect other
people's personal
space on the beach

94

know when high
and low tides are

95

help a group of
strangers by
volunteering to
take a picture
of all of them

96

get your seafood fill at The Crab Trap and/or Smitty's Clam Bar

DID YOU KNOW????
In the 1960's the average price
for shrimp cocktail was $1.25.

97

put your car
windows down
to smell the salt air
while crossing
the bridge

98

soak in Ocean City history at the Historical Museum located in the Community Center

99

debate if there is still treasure on the Sindia wreck

100

whatever you do, don't forget to

_____

i did it

- [ ] 1. grab the brass ring on the carousel and win a free ride
- [ ] 2. enjoy a slice at Manco & Manco's (formerly Mack & Manco) counter and watch the pizza gurus toss the dough
- [ ] 3. take an outside shower
- [ ] 4. win a free game of miniature golf on the last hole
- [ ] 5. crash a Night In Venice party on the bay
- [ ] 6. critique other people's parallel parking skills from your porch
- [ ] 7. confiscate all video games and play a marathon game of Monopoly on a rainy day
- [ ] 8. watch the July 4th fireworks from the beach
- [ ] 9. find a live crab in the rocks on the jetty
- [ ] 10. eat a Jersey tomato
- [ ] 11. have your picture taken on the lifeguard stand at your favorite beach
- [ ] 12. try to finish a large Voltaco's cheese steak by yourself
- [ ] 13. stay inside the green flags on protected beaches
- [ ] 14. fish from the old Longport Bridge
- [ ] 15. ride a surrey cart on the boardwalk and let the youngest take the wheel
- [ ] 16. buy an original piece from an artist at the Boardwalk Art Show
- [ ] 17. test your relationship on a bicycle built for two
- [ ] 18. take a stroll and shop on Asbury Avenue
- [ ] 19. ask them to overflow the bucket at Johnson's Popcorn ("lid off")
- [ ] 20. make a drip castle
- [ ] 21. see the island from the top of the Wonderland Ferris Wheel
- [ ] 22. read all of the boardwalk bench dedications
- [ ] 23. buy a kite at Air Circus on the boardwalk and fly it on the beach
- [ ] 24. forget your age and have fun at the boardwalk rides

- [ ] 25. finish a Kohr Bros. soft serve cone with "jimmies" (yes, they are called jimmies, not sprinkles) before it melts
- [ ] 26. take a surfing lesson
- [ ] 27. arrange for a delivery from Circle Liquor Store
- [ ] 28. explore Ocean City's alleys
- [ ] 29. attempt to save a parking spot on the street using only your body
- [ ] 30. shop the Farmer's Market on Wednesday mornings at the Tabernacle
- [ ] 31. find the perfect shell and bring it home for someone
- [ ] 32. enjoy a warm donut or two from Brown's on the boardwalk
- [ ] 33. lose yourself in a good book on the beach
- [ ] 34. help a stranger save their belongings before getting washed out at high tide
- [ ] 35. keep repeating "I'm on vacation, I'm on vacation" while driving around looking for a parking space
- [ ] 36. find a treasure at a yard sale
- [ ] 37. take the Inn to Inn Tour
- [ ] 38. watch the Baby Parade on the boardwalk (the oldest in the U.S.)
- [ ] 39. try some chicken salad from Bakley's Deli
- [ ] 40. watch them pull the salt water taffy at Shriver's
- [ ] 41. find the "doll houses" on Wovern Place
- [ ] 42. learn to body surf
- [ ] 43. find out the origin of the word "shoobie"
- [ ] 44. race across hot sand without shoes
- [ ] 45. ride a bike from one end of the boardwalk to the other
- [ ] 46. have breakfast overlooking the ocean at Oves
- [ ] 47. walk on the beach in the early morning and be the first to leave footprints in the sand

- [ ] 48. take a photo of the sun rising over the ocean
- [ ] 49. play paddleball or a game of catch by the water
- [ ] 50. take your shoes off and stroll on the beach in the evening
- [ ] 51. take a trolley ride the length of the island
- [ ] 52. bring home a dozen Mallon's sticky buns for the family; that way, *you* get to choose nut, plain, raisin or fruit flavored
- [ ] 53. attend First Night celebration including the fireworks at midnight
- [ ] 54. check out the lagoons via wave runners
- [ ] 55. walk from one end of the boardwalk to the other
- [ ] 56. dig in the dry sand until you reach water or run out of arm
- [ ] 57. find the late Grace Kelly's old family home
- [ ] 58. adopt a hermit crab and name him Hermie
- [ ] 59. start a yearly beach tag collection
- [ ] 60. get creamy fudge from the kettles at Fudge Kitchen
- [ ] 61. spend an hour just people watching on the boardwalk
- [ ] 62. hang out on the porch; leave all electronics inside
- [ ] 63. treat yourself to your favorite junk food on the boardwalk — you're on vacation
- [ ] 64. surf fish from the beach
- [ ] 65. enjoy a toe-tapping musical evening at the Music Pier with the Ocean City Pops
- [ ] 66. protect your lunch on the beach from a seagull attack
- [ ] 67. take a ride on the Haven Avenue bike path
- [ ] 68. introduce yourself to the folks on the porch next door
- [ ] 69. buy ½ price ride tickets on Palm Sunday and Easter Sunday weekends
- [ ] 70. share an order of wings at Charlie's Bar in Somers Point

- [ ] 71. go to the beach with only a towel, a chair and a book
- [ ] 72. peruse the latest selections at Sun Rose Words & Music in town
- [ ] 73. take your dog for a swim at Dog Beach and a romp at the Dog Park
- [ ] 74. walk across the new causeway from Ocean City to Somers Point
- [ ] 75. buy an Ocean City hat or shirt to wear at home
- [ ] 76. catch a sand crab, give it to a little kid and listen to them squeal
- [ ] 77. let the water lap at your ankles as you stand at water's edge and talk with family/friends
- [ ] 78. leave work at home and lose track of what day of the week it is
- [ ] 79. be the first on the beach to spot the dolphins swimming offshore
- [ ] 80. smile and say "Hi" to strangers when they pass
- [ ] 81. attend a church service of a denomination different than your own
- [ ] 82. turn off the a/c, open the windows and feel the ocean breeze
- [ ] 83. visit Ocean City after a snowfall – a true winter wonderland
- [ ] 84. take a nap on the beach
- [ ] 85. wash out a cut or scrape in the ocean while expounding on the healing powers of salt water
- [ ] 86. take a bike ride through the Gardens
- [ ] 87. watch a thunderstorm from the shelter of your porch
- [ ] 88. lose track of time as you walk along the water's edge from beach to beach
- [ ] 89. visit Corson's Inlet State Park in the south end of town
- [ ] 90. say thanks to the lifeguard at the end of your visit

- [ ] 91. take a ½ day fishing trip and try to win the pool
- [ ] 92. eat Jersey sweet corn on the cob and compare it to prior seasons
- [ ] 93. respect other people's personal space on the beach
- [ ] 94. know when high and low tides are
- [ ] 95. help a group of strangers by volunteering to take a picture of all of them
- [ ] 96. get your seafood fill at The Crab Trap and/or Smitty's Clam Bar
- [ ] 97. put your car windows down to smell the salt air while crossing the bridge
- [ ] 98. soak in Ocean City history at the Historical Museum located in the Community Center
- [ ] 99. debate if there is still treasure on the Sindia wreck
- [ ] 100. whatever you do, don't forget to

"I know that everyone who reads this book
will think of something that I absolutely should have
included. Fill in the blank above and DO IT!"
Mary Ann Bolen

about the author

Mary Ann Bolen is a wife, mother, grandmother and retired elementary school teacher who has had Ocean City's sand in her shoes for more than 40 years. She and her husband, Bob, got married in Ocean City, bought their first home in Ocean City and later taught their two children to appreciate the simple, sandy joys of bare feet, front porches and outside showers.

The Bolens live year round in their 105-year-old house. It has been the headquarters "down the Shore" for four generations of relatives and countless friends, and it will always be "home" to Bob, Mary Ann and their now-grown children, Kevin and Mandy.

When she's not reading mystery novels in a beach chair or visiting her children in Key West and Boston, Mary Ann is still checking off the last few items on *The Ocean City Bucket List* and is constantly looking for more of the town's undiscovered gems.

Feel free to add your comments and ideas about the island we all love by emailing maryann.bolen@gmail.com — and always keep some Ocean City sand in your shoes.

Made in the USA
Middletown, DE
13 June 2017